# Joe's Fishing Fiasco:

## Hook, Line, and Ouch!

Marcy Schaaf

# Dedication:

To my brother Joe Schaaf,

Thank you for always being a source of laughter and joy in our family. Your infectious humor and unending positivity brighten even the cloudiest days. This story, like so many of our memories together, is filled with the laughter and love you bring into our lives.

This book was written to be shared with your grandchildren so they may know you a little better and understand the funny and adventurous spirit you always had. Getting a fish hook stuck in your head was a rather common thing that would happen to you, most of the time you would remove it yourself with pliers. But when it was too deep, one of our loving parents would step in to help.

Your ability to turn even the most challenging situations into moments of laughter and resilience is something we all cherish and admire.

With all my love,
Your little sister
Marcy Schaaf

Once upon a time, there was a cheerful teenager named Joe. Joe loved going on fishing trips with his favorite Uncle Bill.

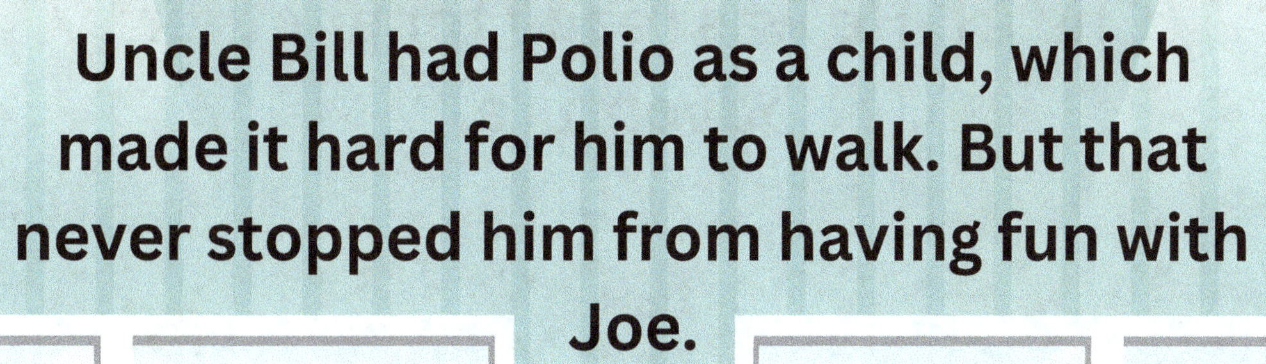

Uncle Bill had Polio as a child, which made it hard for him to walk. But that never stopped him from having fun with Joe.

One sunny morning, Joe rode his bike to Uncle Bill's house with excitement in his heart. He was ready for another adventure.

"Hey Uncle Bill! Ready for some fishing?"
Joe called out, waving enthusiastically.

"You bet, Joe!" Uncle Bill replied, smiling. Joe hooked up the boat to the back of the truck, and off they went.

The nearby lake sparkled under the sun, promising a day filled with fun and fish.

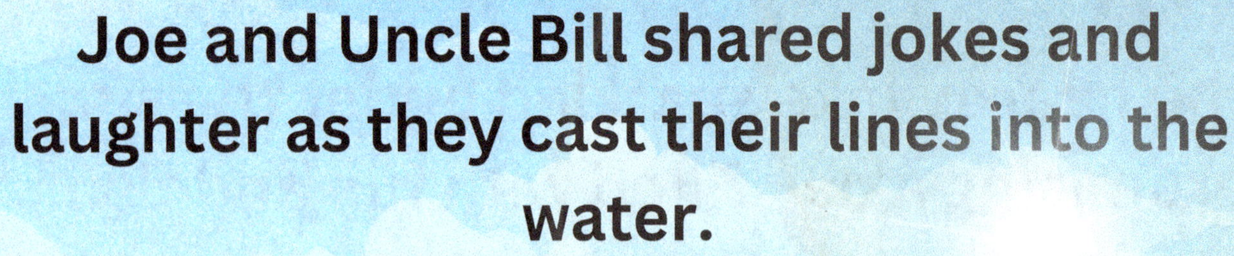

Joe and Uncle Bill shared jokes and laughter as they cast their lines into the water.

Joe felt a tug on his line. "I've got one!" he shouted, reeling in the fish with excitement.

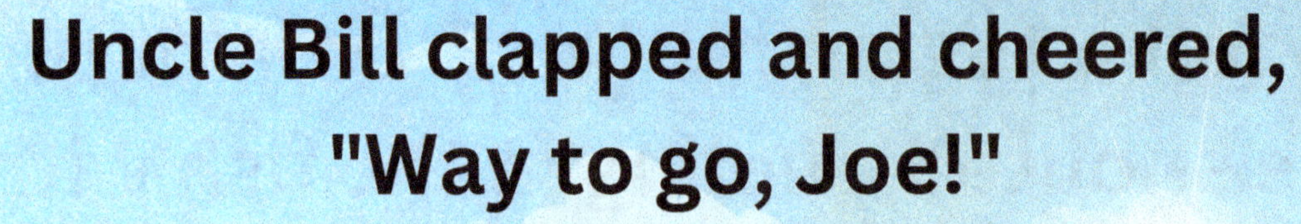

Uncle Bill clapped and cheered,
"Way to go, Joe!"

As the day went on, Joe cast his line once more. But this time, something felt different.

Joe pulled and pulled, but the line wouldn't budge. "Hmm, I think it's stuck," he muttered.

He tugged harder and harder, trying to
free the hook from whatever it was
caught on.

"Careful, Joe," Uncle Bill warned, watching closely.

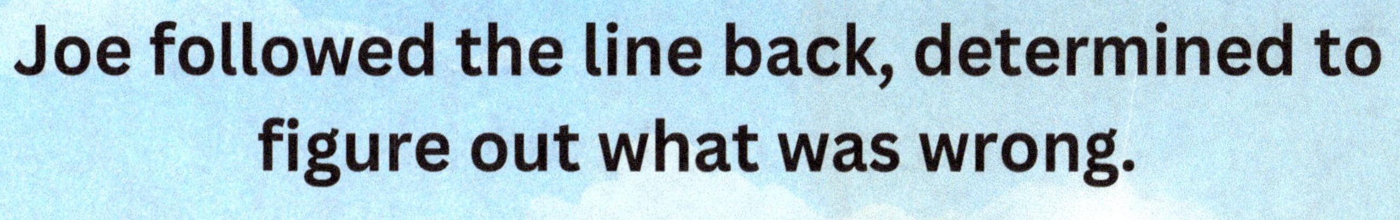

Joe followed the line back, determined to figure out what was wrong.

To his surprise, the hook wasn't caught on
a rock or a branch.
It was stuck in his own head!

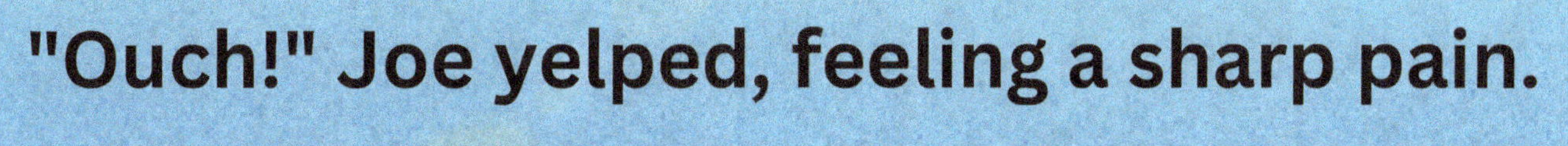

"Ouch!" Joe yelped, feeling a sharp pain.

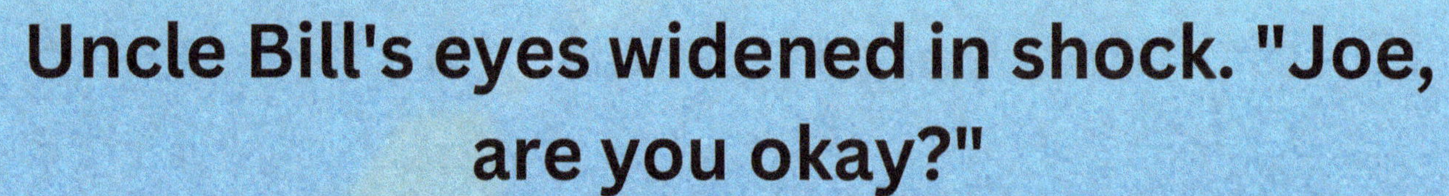

Uncle Bill's eyes widened in shock. "Joe, are you okay?"

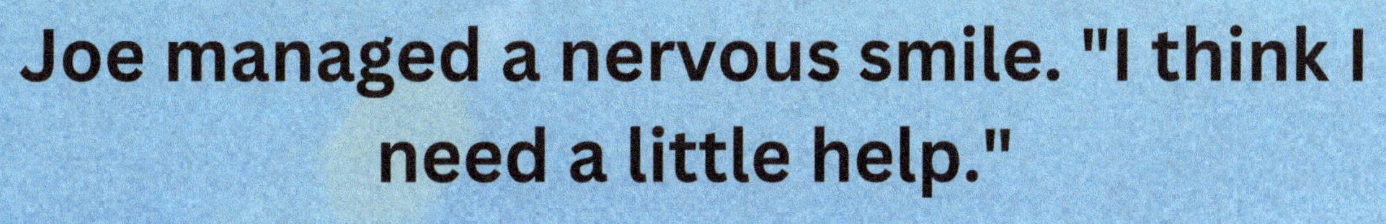

Joe managed a nervous smile. "I think I need a little help."

Joe carefully drove them back home, his
head aching from the hook.

When they arrived, Joe sat on the porch
and called for his mother.

"Mom! I need you!" Joe shouted.

Joe's mother, who was a nurse, rushed out to see what was wrong.

"Oh dear, Joe! What happened?" she asked, examining the hook.

His mother quickly and skillfully removed
the hook from Joe's head.

She cleaned the area well and put in a
quick stitch to close the gap.

"All done," she said, giving Joe a reassuring smile.

"Thanks, Mom," Joe said, feeling much better.

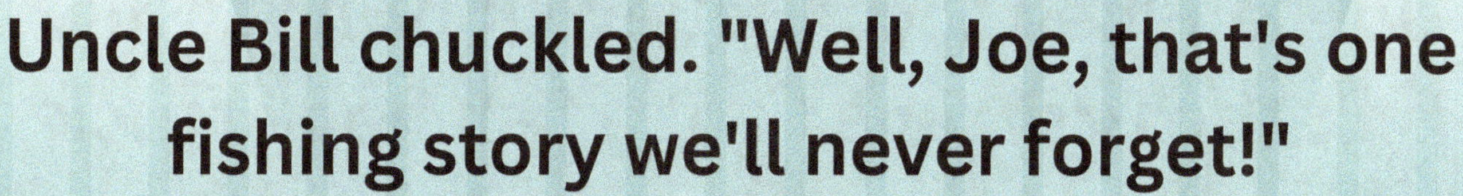

Uncle Bill chuckled. "Well, Joe, that's one fishing story we'll never forget!"

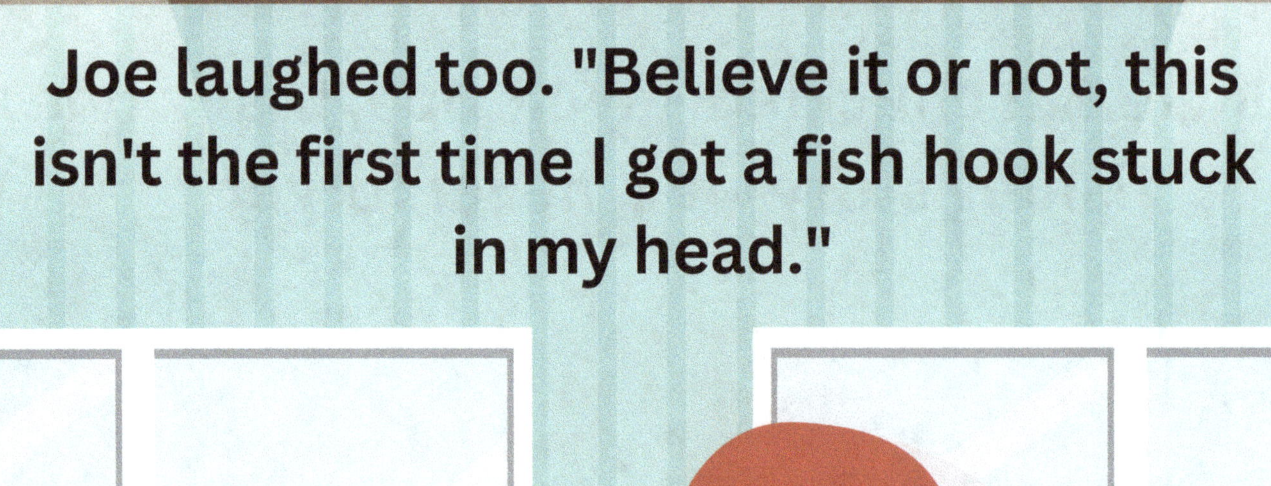

Joe laughed too. "Believe it or not, this isn't the first time I got a fish hook stuck in my head."

Uncle Bill reminded him that sometimes, the best stories come from the most unexpected moments.

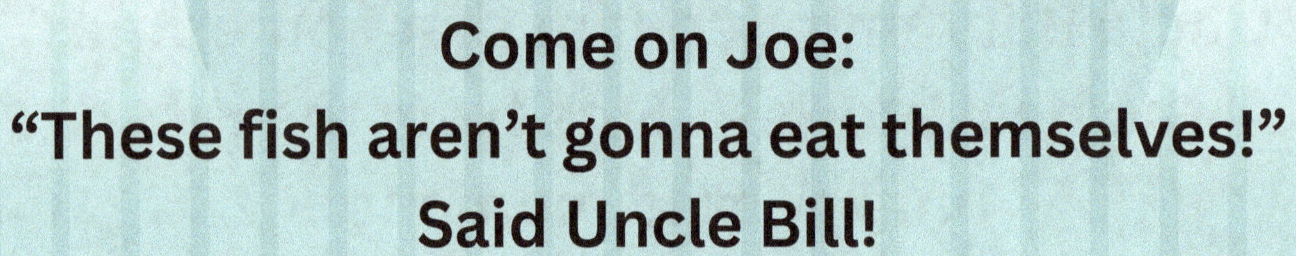
Come on Joe:
"These fish aren't gonna eat themselves!"
Said Uncle Bill!

If you ever get a fish hook stuck in your head, just hope you have a nurse for a mom like Joe!

# The End.

# Books By Schaaf

www.BookBySchaaf.com

Find us at: